CRAFTSMAN'S GUIDES

DECORATIVE PAINT FINISHES

Belinda Hunt

CHARTWELL
BOOKS, INC

To Robert, my first convert

Note: Throughout this book, American terms are signalled in parentheses after their British equivalents the first time in each section they occur.

Editors: Alison Leach and Anne Yelland
Editorial consultant: Fanny Campbell
Editorial assistant: Catherine Tilley
Art director: Elaine Partington
Art editor: David Allen
Designers: Sue Cawson and Su Martin
Illustrator: Graham Bingham
Photography: Jon Bouchier
Studio: Del & Co
Picture research: Liz Eddison

CHARTWELL BOOKS
A division of Book Sales, Inc.
POST OFFICE BOX 7100
114 Northfield Avenue
Edison, N.J. 08818-7100

CLB 4487
© 1995 CLB Publishing, Godalming, Surrey, U.K.
All rights reserved
Printed and bound in Singapore
ISBN 0-7858-0405-6

Contents

Introduction

Many home decorators are unaware of the range of decorative finishes that they could achieve with paint. The skill of generations of painter-craftsmen in using pigment to re-create rare woods and marbles has inspired such awe that the techniques of graining and marbling were long considered too difficult for the amateur to attempt.

Yet many of the techniques involved are easily mastered, provided you are imaginative, patient and careful. It is not necessary to reproduce in convincing detail the meandering grain of burr walnut, for example. It is the overall impression that counts. The earliest exponents of the craft, the ancient Egyptians and Romans, produced unashamedly stylized interpretations. Equally you may be inspired by the examples of graining in the Royal Pavilion, Brighton – the fantasy palace created for George IV when he was Prince Regent. An 18th-century craftsman even conjured up a miniature dragon in his satinwood graining.

The popularity of marbling and graining has waxed and waned, but these techniques were well established by the 18th and 19th centuries, both in Europe and North America. Delightful early examples of marbling from New England date back to 1720. Some techniques have been refined and simplified in the 20th century, with the English designer and decorator, John Fowler, leading the field in the use of transparent paint finishes. He borrowed effects – like dragging – from the woodgrainer, and transformed them into elegant decorative treatments for both walls and furniture.

An adventurous spirit is developing among home decorators, who have become bored by the stark, monochromatic interiors of the sixties and seventies. Colour is all-important. Its versatility and vibrancy is being rediscovered by the use of tinted, transparent glazes and washes. Artists have exploited these techniques for centuries; now decorators are becoming fascinated by broken, translucent colour.

The decorative processes described here will transform the dullest of rooms and the gloomiest of furniture. Coloured glazes can be used to disguise defects, and highlight good proportion and design. Most important of all, they give even the amateur the opportunity to create objects and interiors of great interest and charm.

The bold simplicity of 18th-century American cedar-graining, re-created at the American Museum, Bath.

Paints, glazes and washes

Four principal stages are generally involved in creating
the perfect decorative paint finish. The surface must first
be prepared before the appropriate base coats of paint are
applied. Then the transparent glaze is 'teased' or coaxed
into decorative shape. Finally the surface is protected
with one or more layers of varnish.

Paint falls into two main categories: water- or oil-
based. It is essentially powdered pigment, which gives
colour and opacity, suspended in a binding medium. The
medium determines how the pigment flows and adheres
to the surface and, depending on its ingredients, is
soluble in either water or oil.

Oil- rather than water-based paints are used for most
of the techniques described in this book. Professional
grainers and marblers use both, according to the
demands of the job. For the beginner, oil is the simplest
medium. As base coats, oil paints give the smooth,
non-porous surface vital to a good decorative finish. As
glazes, they are slow to dry, giving you time to work.
They have more body, and therefore hold brush- and
tool-marks more easily than water-based paints.

More preparation is, however, necessary when using
oil paints. The surface must first be protected with a
primer or sealer,   then given three or more base coats

depending on the quality of finish you require. Most oil paints dry with some degree of sheen, but this can be counteracted with a final coat of matt varnish.

Water-based paints are fast-drying and most have a matt finish. They are generally cheaper than oil paints, and smell less strongly. They are easy to use with sprays and rollers, and require less careful brushwork. They need no undercoat and, being porous, can be used on new plaster. They do, however, tend to corrode metals. Some water-based paints may be used on woodwork, but even with a coat of varnish they provide less protection than oil paints.

The real disadvantages arise with washes, as water-based glazes are called. Some techniques, like dragging and stippling, are very difficult to achieve with a quick-drying wash, which requires speed and skill. The paint has to be thinned right down for transparency, leaving it with little body to hold marks made by brushes and rags. The impression is usually softer and more nebulous than similar effects done in oil-based paint. Washes should always be protected with a coat of varnish.

You must decide whether you prefer the cloudy simplicity of a water-based 'rag' to the clear sophistication of an oil-based 'drag'. Whichever you choose, remember one simple rule: oil glazes are best laid over oil-based grounds, washes over water-based grounds. The quality of available paints varies considerably, but it is well worth buying the best you can afford.

Selection of paints and glazes, some of which are familiar from the home-user market, others available only from more specialist outlets.

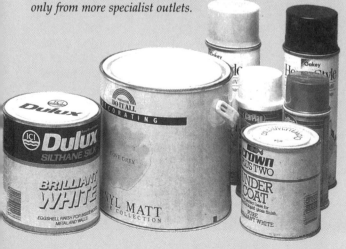

Oil-based paints

Primers, usually oil- or alkyd-based, are used for sealing a porous surface like wood or metal. Different formulations are available for each kind of surface, but there are also good all-purpose primers on the market. Aluminium primers are especially water-resistant; use these on woodwork such as windows or doors that are in contact with damp brickwork or cement.

Undercoat has a high proportion of pigment to medium, making it opaque but quite chalky in texture. It provides the non-porous ground for a subsequent top coat. It may be used as a base for a glaze coat, but the finished surface must be protected with varnish. The colour range is limited, but you can use artist's oils to tint undercoat. Some manufacturers produce a combined primer-undercoat which cuts down the preparation time.

Flat-oil (alkyd flat paint) is regarded by many professionals as the best ground for decorative finishes, but it is only available through specialist suppliers. It dries to a matt finish, has good coverage and handles well. The surface must first be primed and undercoated.

The sponged paint finish of these walls creates an impression of warmth and colour without distracting from the patterns and textures of the upholstery and furniture. The subtle tones can be transformed by using artificial (below) *or natural lighting* (right).

Oil- or alkyd-based eggshell is an excellent substitute for flat-oil, but it has a soft sheen when dry. This can give an added glow to a transparent finish. 'Trade eggshell' is the best in this category of paint, but may be difficult to obtain. There are also 'mid-sheen' oil-based paints which can be used instead of eggshell, but they give less fine a surface. Semi-gloss and gloss paints should not be used; they are designed to resist dirt and grease and so provide insufficient key for a glaze coat.

Water-based paints

Emulsion (latex) is a generic term used to describe a wide variety of water-based paints with finishes ranging from matt to gloss. Tiny globules of synthetic resin, such as vinyl or acrylic, are dispersed through water with pigment and other additives to form an emulsion. Vinyl silks and satins dry with a soft sheen similar to eggshell paint; these are used by some decorators as a base for oil glazes. Vinyl enamels have quite a high degree of gloss.

Cellulose paints

Cellulose paints are used for re-touching the paintwork on cars, and are sold in small aerosol cans. They come in a wide selection of colours and are very useful for stencilling. These paints are extremely toxic, so always wear a mask and make sure the ventilation is good.

Oil glazes

Transparent oil glaze, also called 'scumble' glaze, is a thick, glue-like liquid composed of linseed oil, driers and thinners. A few paint manufacturers still produce commercial oil glaze according to traditional and secret recipes. These glazes are easy to use as they stay 'open' and workable for about 15 minutes, yet are touch-dry within 4–8 hours. Most require tinting, but some are sold in a limited range of colours suitable for woodgraining. Oil glazes can be bought through specialist suppliers, but increasing demand has also persuaded more decorators' (paint) merchants to keep them in stock.

The high linseed oil content can make these glazes yellow with age. Mixing them with eggshell paint and white spirit (paint thinner) reduces the problem.

Undercoat, flat-oil and eggshell can all be thinned with white spirit and used as glazes. They have the advantage of being already tinted; any colour adjustments can be made by adding artist's oils. They are less transparent than oil glaze, and dry more quickly, but there is no problem with yellowing.

Washes

Emulsion paints can be thinned with water and used as a wash. They dry very quickly and do not have the same translucence as oil glazes.

Artist's gouache can be dissolved in water to produce a very clear and luminous wash. Add a little emulsion to give it body.

Oil-based colours

Artist's oils are finely ground pigments bound with linseed oil. They provide a vast colour range and are preferred by most professionals for tinting oil glazes. 'Artist's' quality is more permanent than the 'Student's' range.

Universal stainers, also bound in oil, come in concentrated liquid form and a limited range of colours. They are not as colour-fast as artist's oils.

Signwriter's (japan) colours are bound in quick-drying varnish with little if any oil and so do not strictly belong to this category. They are excellent for stencilling.

Water-based colours

Artist's gouache paints are the most vibrant of the water-based pigments. There is a wide range of colours, and though expensive, they are good for tinting washes.

Artist's acrylics are based on synthetic resins soluble in water. They are fast-drying and useful for stencilling.

Powder colours are just finely ground pigment. They can be used with both water and oil. They can be difficult to dissolve.

Solvents

White spirit (paint thinner), distilled from petrol, should be used to thin all oil-based glazes and paints.

Acetone dissolves cellulose paints, and, in the form of commercial nail varnish (polish) remover, is a good standby if you make a mistake while stencilling.

1 Japan colours; 2 gouache; 3 powder paint; 4 signwriter's colour; 5 universal stainers; 6 oil pigment.

Materials and equipment

Many of the tools and materials used for creating decorative paint finishes are the same as those used for ordinary decoration (painting), but some extra items have to be bought. Both essential tools and materials, and those needed only for specific jobs are listed here.

Stripping

Paint removers, in the form of liquids or pastes, are brushed on, and left to work for a specified time. The dissolved paint is then scraped or rubbed away. They are expensive to use over large areas, but are good for metal surfaces and awkward corners where a blowtorch might be less effective, or where heat might crack nearby glass.

Alkaline paint strippers are extremely powerful and should be used with care. Protect the skin, and use cotton sheeting to cover any surfaces which might be damaged by drips and splashes. Any solvent which remains on the surface will attack subsequent coats of paint, so follow the manufacturer's instructions on washing down and neutralizing the surface.   This is usually done with a

1 Paint kettle;   2 hot-air stripper;   3 shave hook;   4 scraper; 5 paint tin;   6 plastic paint kettle with lid;   7 natural marine sponge;   8 lambswool roller and tray;   9 decorator's brushes.

mixture of water and vinegar. Use brushes with synthetic fibres for applying the stripper as alkaline strippers dissolve natural bristle. Spirit paint removers are expensive, but safer to use.

When using either spirit or alkaline paint removers, good ventilation is essential.

Blowlamps work in a similar way to old-fashioned paraffin (kerosene) lamps. They are fitted with a fuel container, and a nozzle through which the flame is directed. They need constant refilling, which is a disadvantage when stripping large areas. The flame is also liable to go out frequently if inexpertly handled.

A blowtorch has a nozzle-shaped burner attached to a handle, linked to a gas cylinder by a flexible hose. The flame is hotter than that in a blowlamp, and can be regulated, making it more efficient.

Electric paint strippers operate on much the same principle as domestic hair-driers: metal filaments are enclosed in a handpiece and heated up when an electric current flows through them. They may be useful for small areas of delicate mouldings but are painfully slow. Hot-air strippers, in which a fan forces air over the heated element, are far more efficient.

Scrapers have flexible blades of varying widths for use on flat surfaces. For mouldings and recesses, use a shave-hook with a straight-sided triangular head, or one with both straight and curved edges.

Abrasives

Abrasive papers are used to rub down surfaces at almost every stage, from preparation to the final coat of varnish. Abrasive particles – of glass, flint, garnet, aluminium oxide or silicon carbide – are glued to backing paper of different kinds. The papers are graded by letter or number, or both, according to the coarseness of the particles. Different systems of grading are used, but as a general guide the letters used to grade particles are S (strong), C (coarse), M (medium) and F (fine). The quality of backing paper is denoted by A, for hand-rubbing, and D, a tougher paper which is also used with sanding machines. In the numerical system of grading, the higher the number, the coarser the grit. This is the most widely used system and measures the grade by the number of holes per square inch through which the abrasive particles would pass.

1 Wire wool; 2 sugar soap; 3 knotting; 4 paint-remover gel;
5 fine surface filler; 6 flexible abrasive block; 7 cork block;
8 abrasive papers; 9 filler knife; 10 putty knife;
11 silicon carbides.

A useful selection for most purposes would be 30/40/60 (coarse), 100/120 (medium) and 150/250 (fine). It is worth spending a little more on garnet papers for the preparation work as the cheaper glass (sand) papers clog up quickly and disintegrate.

For rubbing down between coats, use silicon carbide (wet and dry) papers. They can be moistened with water or linseed oil, to improve the cutting action and reduce the dust in the atmosphere. If rinsed out regularly in water while you work, these papers will last longer than other varieties. The finest grades of silicon carbide paper, 400/600 and 1200, are used to achieve a flawlessly polished, professional finish. Self-lubricating papers are also available, which require no rinsing.

Steel wool is more flexible than abrasive paper and may be better for the more inaccessible areas of moulded or carved surfaces. Grades range from 3 (coarse) to 0000 (very fine).

Abrasive powders and polishes are used for the finishing touches. Powdered pumice or rottenstone is rubbed over the surface with a lubricant such as linseed oil. Rottenstone is the finer of the two. Car polishes like T-Cut, household brass polish or toothpaste may be used. Perfectionists achieve a final burnish using ordinary flour.

Preparing the surface

Fillers will be needed for repairing cracks and holes, and for smoothing over uneven surfaces. Use all-purpose, cellulose or vinyl-based fillers – ready-mixed or in powder form – for the deeper splits. The fine-grain fillers are for hairline cracks and minor irregularities like raised woodgrain.

A putty knife has a pointed blade, combining both a curved and straight edge. It is rigid enough to press the filler in firmly, yet makes a flexible scraper for smoothing off the surface afterwards.

Knotting, composed of shellac and methylated spirit (wood alcohol), is used for sealing knots in wood to prevent resin from discolouring subsequent layers of paint.

Sugar soap crystals, dissolved in water, provide a powerful, silicon-free cleaning agent for surfaces before painting.

Brushes

Standard decorator's brushes are made of natural bristle or synthetic fibre. Hogshair bristle is undoubtedly the best. The tapered hairs are split at the ends into 'flags', producing a fine, soft tip for perfect 'laying off'. Cheaper brushes are filled with horsehair, synthetic fibre or a mixture of both. They are less densely filled, so lose shape more easily. As with paint, it is worth buying good brushes to obtain an expert finish.

Use wide, flat brushes for walls: 100mm (4in.), or 125mm (5in.) if you have a strong wrist. Keep a selection of narrower brushes for woodwork: 75mm (3in.) and 50mm (2in.) for most surfaces, and a 25mm (1in.) 'cutting in tool' for corners and edges. One set should be reserved for white paint, another for colours. If your budget allows, have a third set for glazes.

Dust brushes or jamb dusters are excellent for cleaning off surfaces before painting, and can also be used for stippling.

Varnish brushes should be kept immaculately clean and never used for any other purpose. Buy the best quality decorator's brushes for varnishing, or the traditional oval varnish brush which has more bristles for smoother application. Different widths are available.

1 Flat varnish brushes (gliders, dragging brushes); **2, 3** *fitches;* **4** *mop;* **5** *overgrainer;* **6** *mottler;*

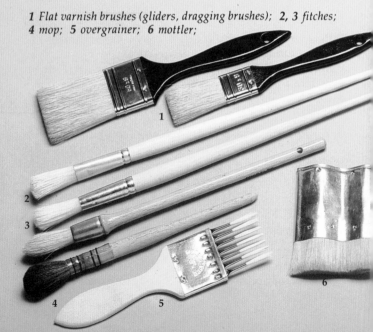

Specialist equipment and brushes

Numerous ingenious devices have been developed over the centuries as the techniques involved in marbling and woodgraining became more sophisticated. Many are expensive, but you can improvise and still get realistic and impressive results.

Badger softeners are used to blur and blend glaze colours in marbling and woodgraining. They are the elite of specialist brushes and are priced accordingly. A hogshair softener or dust brush may be used instead.

Graining brushes have thin rows of bristle, which vary in length and texture according to the brush. Floggers, with long flexible bristles, produce narrow parallel lines like a coarse woodgrain. Widths range from 50mm (2in.) to 225mm (9in.). The bristles of draggers and overgrainers are shorter and finer, and the narrower widths – from 10mm (⅜in.) – are useful for furniture. Standard decorator's brushes can also be used for graining, particularly the coarse-haired emulsion (latex) brushes.

The mottler's curving edge is used by woodgrainers to create irregular highlights.

7 jamb duster; 8 oval varnish brush; 9 badger softener; 10 hogshair softener.

Stipplers are like pads of bristle, or rubber spines, used to distribute glaze evenly over a surface. Sizes vary from 100mm × 25mm (4in. × 1in.) to 300mm × 300mm (12in. × 12in.). Rubber stipplers are cheaper than bristle ones but less durable, and produce a coarser pattern.

Fitches may be round or flat; the bristles are attached to a long handle like an artist's brush. Use them for dabbing on colour and stippling over small areas. Mops are similar, but made of softer hair.

Swordliners, used by signwriters, can be twisted and twirled through the glaze to simulate the veins in marble. The soft hairs, usually of sable, are cut diagonally to a fine point.

Artist's brushes are always useful for fine details in graining and marbling. Squirrel and camel hair are adequate for most decorative painting and are considerably cheaper than the finest quality sable.

Marine (natural) sponges are used to produce imitation granite and other mottled effects. Synthetic sponges are more rigid, and give a hard-edged pattern which can be irritating to the eye.

1 Large stipple brush; 2 small stipple brush; 3,4 heartgrainers; 5 rubber comb; 6 combination rubber comb; 7 artist's brushes; 8 swordliners.

Goose feathers are the traditional veining tool for marbling.

Combs used for graining are made of metal or rubber, with even or graduated teeth.

Heartgrainers are curved rubber or plastic stamps, the head incised with a pattern like the heartgrain in pine or oak.

Painting equipment

Paint kettles (buckets) may be of plastic or metal. It helps to keep your paint clean if you pour small amounts into a kettle as you need it, leaving the bulk in the covered paint tin (can). Plastic kettles with lids (for the 2.5 litre / ½ gal. or 1 litre/¼ gal. sizes) are useful if you want to store paint or glaze for short periods.

Paint trays should be sloping and wide enough to take your roller. They should hold enough paint to coat the roller easily. The base should have ridges to scrape off excess paint from the roller. Trays can be of plastic or metal.

Rollers are used on large areas, with oil- and water-based paints. Many decorators (painters) prefer them to brushes; they are quicker and, some argue, give a finer finish. You will, however, need brushes for getting into corners. Originally lambswool was used to cover the roller head but synthetic fibres are now more common. The pile may be short, medium or long; the shorter the pile, the smoother the finish. Extension rods can be attached to the handle for painting ceilings and high walls.

Spray guns 'atomize' the paint under pressure, breaking it up into tiny particles which are then sprayed over the surface in a fine mist. They reduce the painting time, especially over large areas, and when handled by an expert, simplify furniture painting which is laborious when done with a brush. Beginners may have problems. All the parts must be scrupulously clean, the paint thinned to the right consistency, and the spraying action must be fluid and constant. Areas which are not to be painted, such as windows and doors, must be carefully masked. Unless you propose to use spray guns frequently and can learn to master the technique, they are best avoided.

Stencilling

A firm surface is essential for cutting stencils, preferably one which will not score, snagging the blade as you cut. A sheet of glass is the best backing to work on, or a self-repairing plastic cutting mat, obtainable from artist's suppliers.

If you are making your own stencils, get a supply of stencil board or acetate from an artist's supplier, a craft knife and masking tape. Carbon and tracing paper will also come in useful.

Spray mount (re-positioning glue), used by graphic designers for fixing lay-outs, helps to keep stencils in place.

Stencil brushes have short, stubby bristles designed for dabbing or 'pouncing' colour through stencils.

Miscellany

Cotton rag is needed in large quantities for ragged finishes. It should be lint-free. Synthetic fabrics are less absorbent than cotton.

Fine mutton-cloth (muslin or cheese cloth) is useful for cleaning off surplus glaze.

Tack rags are lint-free cloths impregnated with a 'tacky' substance like wax, and are used for removing dust from a surface before painting. You can make your own by soaking a cotton cloth – an old handkerchief is ideal – in warm water. Wring it out and sprinkle with white spirit (paint thinner). Pour 3 teaspoons of oil- or alkyd-based varnish on to the cloth, wring it out again and hang it up to dry for 30 minutes. Keep it in a screw-top jar, and just repeat the process when it dries out.

Vinegar is mixed with water to provide the glaze coat in some graining techniques.

Metallic powders, in imitation of gold, silver and bronze, give added lustre to stencils and exotic marbles. Specialist suppliers also stock transfer metal – gold or Dutch metal (a cheap substitute), silver, aluminium and platinum in leaf form – pressed between tissue sheets.

Jam jars (jelly glasses) or other small containers are needed for mixing colours. Glass and metal are best as some plastics will melt on contact with white spirit.

Cardboard, of the thickness used for face tissue boxes, is used for some marbling and graining techniques.

Empty paint tins (cans) are invaluable for disposing of slops and glaze-soaked rags.

Whiting consists of finely powdered chalk and has many uses, from priming canvas to making putty. When rubbed over a glossy surface like varnish, it provides a key for the next coat.

Gold size is a quick-drying synthetic varnish used as an adhesive for metal leaf.

Varnishes are described in detail on pp. 72-5.

Care of equipment

Rollers should be rinsed thoroughly in cold water (or white spirit if you are using oil-based paints), then washed in warm water and washing-up (dishwashing) liquid. Rinse them out and hang from a hook to dry.

Follow the same procedure for brushes. It is a good idea to drill a hole in the brush handle so that you can hang it up. If paint has hardened on the bristles, soak them in a proprietary cleaner, but never stand a brush on its bristles – they will be twisted permanently out of shape. Pass a thin stick or wire through the hole drilled in the handle and suspend the brush in a jar of liquid cleaner, so that the bristles are submerged but not resting on the bottom.

New brushes should be twirled between both palms to shake out any loose hairs, rinsed out in white spirit and twirled once more until dry. Store brushes flat, wrapped in newspaper.

Rinse specialist brushes in the appropriate solvent and wash them in soapy water. Traces of white spirit left in bristle brushes or rubber combs damage them, so wash and rinse them until you can no longer smell any spirit.

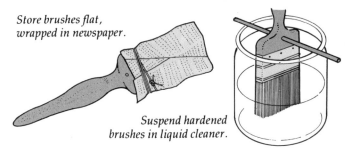

Store brushes flat, wrapped in newspaper.

Suspend hardened brushes in liquid cleaner.

Preparation

The first lesson a craftsman learns is the importance of good preparation. No decorative finish will survive if the surface beneath it is unsound, and marbling or graining executed over visible brushmarks, or dust particles, looks absurd. The groundwork may seem tedious, but persevere. You will be rewarded by the end result.

Make sure that the surface is dry and problem-free. Ask your builders' merchant (paint supplier) for advice on dealing with fungus, crumbling plaster, damp or chemically active surfaces. If you are painting a room, remove the curtains and light furniture; heavy items can be left in the centre of the room, covered with polythene or cotton sheeting. Remove the carpet if you can; otherwise protect it with polythene, then cover with heavy-duty cotton dust-sheets to absorb any spilled paint. You will need a stepladder for painting walls. For ceilings you will need two, to support a scaffold board so that you can move along as you paint.

Old surfaces

Wash down the surface with a mild solution of sugar soap and warm water. Apply it with an old brush, working from the bottom upwards to avoid dirty streaks forming over dry surfaces below as they can be hard to remove. Rinse thoroughly with clean water and wipe with a sponge or chamois leather. Allow to dry completely before painting.

Areas of blistered or flaking paint on wood, plaster and metal, must be removed with a scraper, and then rubbed down with abrasive paper. Choose your abrasive paper to suit the condition of the surface; if it is too coarse you will scratch the surface still further. Uneven paintwork, like brush-marks and drips, can be smoothed down with a grade 150 or 240 silicon carbide (wet and dry), moistened with water. Finish off with a grade 320 or 400. For flat surfaces tear a standard sheet, 275mm × 225mm (11in. × 9in.), in four, and wrap one quarter around a sanding block. You can make your own out of a block of wood faced with felt, or buy one of cork or rubber from a builders' merchant (hardware store). Rub down any moulded surfaces with smaller strips, held between your fingers and thumb.

Removing wallpaper

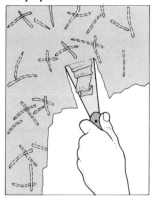

1 Scratch surface of washables so that water penetrates glue. *2 After soaking, remove paper with a wide scraper.*

After rubbing down, wipe the surface clean with a damp cloth. This will be sufficient preparation for most emulsioned surfaces. Polished woodwork should be wiped over with white spirit (paint thinner) to remove traces of wax, before abrading.

Painting over old wallpaper can present problems. If the original glue is weak, the additional weight of new paint may pull the paper from the wall. Some of the inks used in patterned wallpapers will 'bleed' through paint applied over them. If the wallpaper is at all unsound, strip if off completely using a scraper, with the aid of a steam-stripper or boiling kettle if it proves tough. Soaking the paper first may be enough.

If the paper is still firmly attached, dust down the walls with a soft brush and seal them with an all-purpose primer. If the paper is liable to bleed, use an aluminium primer. You can also cross-line the walls, applying the lining paper horizontally. Remember that too much moisture, from washing or sizing, will swell the old paper and weaken the original glue still further.

If large areas of previous paintwork are unsound, it is best to strip the whole surface. This also applies to varnished surfaces, even those in good condition, as they are notoriously resistant to paint. Once stripped, treat old surfaces as new.

The method you use for stripping will depend on the type of paint and surface. In some older houses you may find distemper on ceilings and decorative plasterwork.

The powdery texture of distemper will undermine any paint you put on top, so remove it by scouring down the surface with water and a stiff brush. When dry, seal the surface with an alkali-resisting primer or proprietary sealer.

You may be able to remove some areas of peeling paint with a scraper alone; if not, you will need to do so with heat or chemicals. Heat-stripping is the least laborious and expensive method for large areas, and is best suited to removing oil paint from woodwork. It is inefficient if the surface conducts heat, and dangerous near rotten wood which may ignite.

A blowtorch is easier to use than a blowlamp, and a hot-air stripper is safer than either, as there is no naked flame. On flat surfaces work from the bottom upwards, letting the heat soften the paint, and then scrape it off with a stripping knife (scraper). Use a shave hook on moulded surfaces, working from top to bottom. Be careful not to play the flame or hot air over one area for too long, as you may scorch the wood. Paint will not adhere to charred wood, so damaged areas must be removed by rubbing down. After stripping, smooth off the whole surface with abrasive paper.

Always remember that there is a real danger of fire when using any heat-stripping equipment. You must take every precaution. Remove all inflammable materials

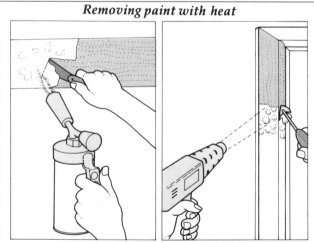

Removing paint with heat

Use a hand-held gas torch for large flat areas. Hot-air strippers are safer; use a shave hook for mouldings.

such as curtains, books and papers. Put burnt paint in an empty tin and check that it is not smouldering. Keep a careful eye on flying sparks. Direct the nozzle away from any surface if you need to pause; better still, turn the machine off.

Have a bucket of water or sand to hand in case of accidents. If you need to protect the floor, kitchen foil (aluminium foil) provides a good shield.

If you are stripping metal or plaster, or areas near glass, you will have to use chemical paint strippers. Check with your local decorators' merchant (paint store) which kind – spirit or alkali – is suitable for the job. The chemical is painted on to the surface, using a brush with synthetic fibres, and left until the paint bubbles up and can be removed easily with a scraper. Follow the manufacturer's instructions on cleaning the surface afterwards. Some chemical strippers lift the grain on timber, which must be rubbed down before painting.

Safety precautions are again of utmost importance. These chemicals can burn very badly, so cover your skin and protect your face and eyes with a mask if working on areas overhead. Keep the container closed when not in use, and well away from children and pets. You will need good ventilation, and you must be careful not to create sparks or flame when using spirit-based removers as they are highly inflammable.

Removing paint with chemicals

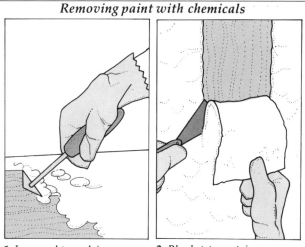

1 Leave gel to soak in, remove with a shave hook.

2 Blanket-type strippers remove many layers at a time.

New surfaces

Plaster surfaces should be completely dry before you decorate (paint) them with oil-based paints. The alkalis active in wet plaster will react with the drying oils in paint. In new houses plaster can take up to a year to dry completely. Test by wetting the surface with water and holding a piece of red litmus paper against it. If the paper goes blue, the chemicals are still active. You can, however, use emulsions (latex) and water-based paints; they allow moisture to escape from the plaster. If the plaster is dry, remove any efflorescence – powdery salt deposits on the surface – with a cloth or brush. Do not wash them off; the moisture will only reactivate them.

Remove any nibs of plaster with a scraper; abrasive paper will scratch the surface. Make good any holes and cracks with a plaster filler, and coat with an alkali-resisting primer if you are going to use oil-based paints.

Lining paper provides the finest surface for painting on walls. It means more work, but the final result is smoother than painted plaster. The plaster should first be sized – painted with a weak solution of wallpaper glue – and allowed to dry before the walls are papered. Butt-join the edges to avoid vertical ridges, which would show up under paint. For oil paints the paper must then be sealed with a glue size solution or thinned emulsion paint. Some professionals omit this stage completely and use an acrylic combined primer/undercoat. The import-

Knotting and filling

1 *Seal knots in new wood with knotting.*

2 *Press filling into deep cracks with a putty knife.*

ant point is to provide a barrier between the paper and any oil-based paint.

Make sure that all nails on bare wood surfaces have been punched below the surface. Rub wood down dry with abrasive paper as moisture will raise the grain. Make good any cracks and holes, and use a fine surface filler to fill the grain. Seal knots with a coat or two of knotting, or remove them completely with a chisel and mallet, filling the holes afterwards. Always prime new wood, to provide a good key for the base coats. Brush the primer well into the wood. Use aluminium primer on hardwoods and resinous softwoods like pitch pine.

Even new metal surfaces may have rust spots and will need scraping with a wire brush. Wipe the surface with white spirit to remove any grease and prime with a proprietary metal primer.

Stopping and filling

Large holes and cracks are 'stopped' with a stiff compound compatible with the surface. Hairline cracks, small indentations and open-grain timbers are 'filled' with a finer paste composed of various substances – for example, plaster, cellulose and cement – bound with oil, water, resin or cellulose medium. For deep cracks in wood use an oil stopper, and plaster for walls and ceilings. Scrape out any loose material and press the stopping into the gap with a putty knife. With plaster it may be necessary to cut back the edges if they are crumbling, and to wet the crevice to bind the stopper. It is better to build up the stopper in layers, allowing each to dry before the next is laid and finishing just below the surface. A fine surface filler, which is more easily rubbed down, can then be used to bring it level with the surface. There are also specially formulated stoppers for metal.

If any irregularities remain, a fine surface filler should be used to ensure a totally smooth finish. All-purpose fillers are available in powder form or ready-mixed, and they can also be used as stoppers if the cracks are not too deep. They are spread over the surface with a putty knife and then rubbed down. There are several proprietary fillers on the market, including oil-based 'rubbing' or 'grain' filler, which is applied with a cloth.

Minor surface defects are stopped and filled after priming, to give a better key. Many of these putties and pastes will absorb paint, so touch them up with primer or undercoat before applying the next coat of paint.

Painting the base coats

Wipe the lid of the paint tin (can) before opening it. Stir the paint (unless it is of the non-drip or 'thixotropic' variety). If the tin has been opened before, a skin may have formed on the surface. Cut it out cleanly with an old knife, stir and then strain the paint into a kettle.

If you are decorating an entire room, the sequence should be ceiling, walls and woodwork. Always finish one whole area – ceiling, wall, or run of skirting board (baseboard) – in a single session, to avoid creating obvious joins where one section meets another. Paint in panels of about 100cm × 50cm (40in. × 20in.), blending one section into another. Start walls at the top right-hand corner (or left, if you are left-handed) and ceilings near a window.

The base coats may be applied with a roller, brush or spray-gun. If using a roller, first paint the corners using a 25mm (1in.) brush. Fill one third of your paint tray with paint, dip in the roller, rub it over the ribs on the base of the tray to remove excess paint and roll it over the surface. Use diagonal strokes initially, finishing off with straight strokes. Be firm but not vigorous; if the roller spins off the surface, it will shower you with paint.

When using a brush, pour small amounts of paint at a time into a kettle, and keep the paint tin covered. Dip the tip of the brush into the paint, covering no more than an inch of bristle, and press it against the inside of the kettle, not the rim. Working in sections, apply the paint with vertical strokes, brush in with horizontal strokes and 'lay

Preparing paint

1 Cut skin cleanly with a knife.

2 Strain through nylon mesh into a kettle.

Applying paint by roller

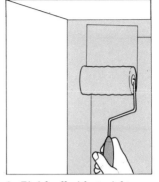

1 *Paint corners with a brush then apply diagonal strokes.*

2 *Finish off with straight roller strokes.*

Applying paint by brush

1 *Press bristles gently against inside of kettle.*

2 *On woodwork, lay off in the direction of the grain.*

off' lightly with a vertical stroke once more. On wood, lay off following the direction of the grain.

Spray guns are not for beginners and it would be wise to see them demonstrated before using them yourself. If you are determined to try, mask off all the areas you do not want to paint. The spray can reach further than you intend. Wear a mask and ensure good ventilation. Thin the paint according to the manufacturer's instructions. Holding the nozzle about 300mm (12in.) away from the surface, keep it moving to prevent drips forming. It should always be held on a plane parallel with the surface to ensure the paint film is even.

Masking before spraying

Use masking tape and newspaper to cover areas such as light switches or skirting boards which you do not want to spray.

Water-based decorative finishes will need one or two base coats of emulsion, depending on the porosity of the surface, or if the colour to be covered is very dark. For new plaster, the emulsion for the first coat should be thinned with an equal quantity of water. A 2.5 litre (½ gal.) tin should cover about 35 sq.m (42 sq.yd) and be sufficiently dry to re-coat in 4–6 hours.

Oil-based finishes will need three base coats after the primer has been applied. As a first coat you may use undercoat, which has excellent opacity. A 2.5 litre (½ gal.) tin will cover 40 sq.m (48 sq.yd) and be ready to paint over in 12–16 hours. Follow this by two coats of flat-oil or eggshell, which have similar spreading capacity to undercoat. Allow flat-oil an additional 8 hours to dry before re-coating. If opacity is not important for the first coat, just use three coats of flat-oil or eggshell. It is important to rub down the surface between coats, using a grade 400 silicon carbide paper, lubricated with water.

For small items of furniture, the whole process of preparation can be circumvented by spraying the surface with cellulose paint, sold in aerosol cans as car sprays. Each coat dries within 30 minutes, and a smooth, hard surface can be built up by applying several layers of paint, rubbing down between coats. Any filling must be done with a nitro-cellulose filler. The disadvantage of cellulose paint is its brittleness which may lead to cracking.

Spraying

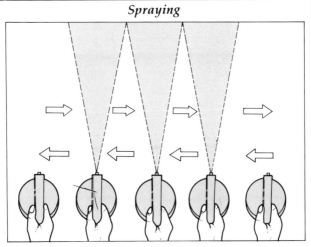

1 *Continue the movement of spraying with the gun off at the beginning and end of a run to avoid colour build up.*

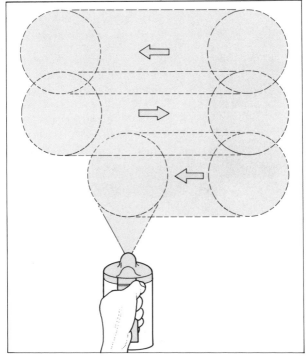

2 *Overlap the edges of each stroke by about a third – the spray fan is thinner at the extremities.*

Broken colour

Having prepared the surface meticulously, you can now enjoy the creative aspects of decorative paint finishes. You may have decided on your colour, selecting a tone to match the curtains, a picture, or a rug. Before you commit yourself, take time to practise with different colours and techniques. Until you do so, it is difficult to imagine the variations in tone and texture that can be achieved.

You are now working with reflected light, rebounding off the pale colour of the base coat and filtering back through a transparent film of colour – like white sand shimmering through blue water. The base colour can be revealed still further by breaking up or 'distressing' the glaze, with brushes, sponges, rags, combs or even your daily newspaper. You draw a fine veil over the surface, and can then change its colour and texture at will.

Decorative techniques using glazes fall roughly into two categories: glaze is added or subtracted in some way – sponged on or sponged off, brushed on or dragged off. This is where practice is important, as some techniques are less suited to particular areas than others. Ragging and sponging can look blotchy over mouldings, blurring the line they were meant to define. The delicate appeal of stippling, while subtle on furniture, may be too bland for your taste when used on a large wall. Most hardware shops sell coated hardboard (masonite) – sprayed with white eggshell paint – in a range of sizes. This makes a cheap ground for practice, as you can always wipe off the glaze with white spirit (paint thinner) and try again.

Colour is the joy, and the bane, of the decorator's (painter's) craft. When you get it right, the pleasure is supreme, but it may have taken many hours to achieve. Here too your practice boards will be invaluable. You can experiment with colour, and by moving the boards around the room, actually see how the tone changes with the light. Try creating the colour you want by building up layers of glaze. A soft pink followed by a pale primrose will give you peach, of a delicacy and depth which no flat paint can rival. Use pale glazes over dark to reproduce the clouded elegance of old frescoes, or progressively darker tones of the same colour to build up intensity of colour. Try out the effect on one wall to get a better impression. It will stay soft enough to remove with white spirit for at least 20 minutes, depending on the consistency.

Left: *Sponged walls and dragged woodwork – using different thicknesses of glaze – produce subtle shades of a single colour.*

Mixing colours

Skill in mixing colours will come with practice. Most professionals are less concerned with the theory than the 'feel' for a colour. When matching and blending, learn to look through half-closed eyes. You will begin to see the subtle emphasis of red, or blue, or yellow which distinguishes, for example, one grey from another.

Start with a limited palette – the selection of artist's oils and gouache is enormous. As you become more confident, experiment with different colours. You will find the following colours adequate initially:

Reds   rose madder, vermilion, burnt sienna
Greens   terre-verte, viridian
Blues   Prussian blue, French ultramarine
Yellows   lemon yellow, cadmium yellow, raw sienna

Burnt and raw umber are useful additions; they are deep earth browns, the first with a reddish cast, the latter with an undertone of green. They are good for 'muddying' other colours, adding warmth or toning them down. Ivory black is the most transparent of the blacks and so is the best for glazes. Zinc or Chinese white should also be included on your list.

A little knowledge of colour theory can cut down the time you spend on mixing colours. It is helpful to know that complementary colours – red/green, yellow/purple, blue/orange – have a sobering effect on each other. If your red is too brilliant, add a little green and you reduce the garishness instantly. Similarly, the softest greys are made by mixing equal quantities of two complementary colours; this is far more subtle than a blend of black and white.

Most decorative paint finishes look best over a white or cream ground, especially if the glaze itself is pale. But do not be inhibited from trying out coloured grounds. You can get very striking effects with a glaze distressed over a ground of similar colour, but a paler or darker shade.

Mixing water-based glazes

It is important when making up your glaze to mix more than you might need. It is difficult, if not impossible, to make up the same colour again. As a rough guide, assume you will need half the quantity of the paint used for a single base coat. Mix your glaze in a large plastic bucket or paint kettle, and then strain it into another through a pair of old nylon tights to filter out any un-dissolved pigment or dirt.

For a water-based glaze or wash, use emulsion (latex) thinned with water – up to 80% water to 20% paint for a high degree of translucency. It will never, however, be as transparent as an oil-based glaze. Use commercial colours, or tint a white emulsion with gouache paints, dissolved first in a little water.

For a really luminous wash, simply dissolve a little gouache in water. Add some emulsion – no more than 3 tablespoons to 1 litre (¼ gal.) of tinted water – to give body. This glaze is too thin for techniques like dragging and stippling, and is used principally for colour-washing. Acrylics can be used instead of gouache, but they are expensive.

The drawback in using water-thinned paints for dec-orative finishes is the speed at which they dry. The problem can be alleviated slightly if you use a less porous base coat, for example, vinyl silk rather than emulsion.

Oil glazes

The simplest glaze to use is commercial oil glaze, thinned with white spirit. Start with equal quantities of glaze and white spirit, adding more spirit if you prefer a thin, less textured finish. Oil glaze tends to yellow with age, so add some white oil-based undercoat or eggshell to counteract discoloration. Two tablespoons per litre (¼ gal.) of glaze is adequate. If you find a commercial

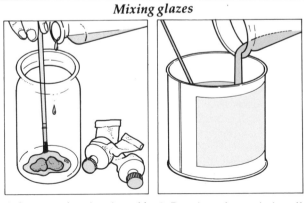

Mixing glazes

1 *Squeeze colour into jar; add solvent.*

2 *Pour into glaze, stirring all the time.*

eggshell paint in the colour you want, you can miss out the tinting stage and simply combine the glaze, eggshell paint and white spirit in equal quantities. Some blue pigments, when mixed with glaze, are particularly prone to yellowing, so choose a commercially tinted eggshell paint closest to the shade you want, and make any necessary adjustments yourself with artist's oils.

Pour the glaze and white eggshell paint into a large paint kettle. Use a small container, like a jam jar (jelly glass), for tinting. Squeeze the artist's oils into the jar, add a little white spirit and dissolve the paint – an artist's old paintbrush is ideal for stirring. (Universal stainers need no dissolving.) Pour the colour into the glaze, stirring all the time. Keep adding more colour until you have the shade you want; test it on the relevant surface, as glaze always looks darker in the kettle. When you are satisfied with the colour, add white spirit to thin the glaze, a little at a time, until it has the consistency of single (thin) cream. Try working with this, but thin it still further if you find it too sticky to work with. Remember, however, that adding white spirit speeds up the drying time.

Eggshell and undercoat can be thinned with equal quantities of white spirit to make a glaze, and tinted in the same way as oil glaze. This makes a less transparent mixture, and is faster drying.

With all decorative paint finishes, make sure you complete a specific area, whether it is a door panel or an entire wall, in one session. Joins can never be hidden if you try to merge wet glaze into a dry edge.

Colour-washing

The decorative painter has borrowed a trick from the water-colourist: using thin washes to create soft impressions of colour, adding layer upon layer of translucent paint for greater depth. This technique imparts a nebulous bloom of colour, flattering even to the roughest wall. The technique is not suited to woodwork and furniture as the wash would be difficult to control over small areas.

Have a supply of rags for wiping up spatters, and a soft brush or sponge for catching drips as you paint. The surface must be absorbent, so use matt emulsion for your base coat. Wipe the wall down with a water and vinegar solution to remove any grease, rinse it and allow to dry.

Make up a thin wash of emulsion or gouache, diluted

Use loose, random strokes in colour-washing, mopping up any drips with a sponge or rag.

with water. Paint it on to the wall with a wide, flat brush, using generous, sweeping strokes, moving in all directions. You will need to work fast to stop the wash flowing down the wall. Keep a soft brush or sponge in your other hand, catching drips and blending them into the surface.

A single coat painted in this way can appear very ragged and uneven. A second application, of the same or another colour, will help to soften the effect. Allow the first wash to dry completely; leave it overnight if possible. This lessens the risk of dissolving the first coat when you apply the second. Washes of thinned acrylic paints are the safest as they dry to a tough finish, unaffected by water.

Colour-washing can also be done with oil-based undercoat or eggshell, thinned with up to 90% white spirit, but the effect is more uniform. The base coat should be oil-based too.

Sponging

You can create more varied effects with sponging than with almost any other decorative technique, yet it is the simplest. The sponge can be used to dab colour on, or pressed into wet glaze to take it off. One colour can be sponged over another, when the first coat is dry for a crisp impression, or when it is wet for a cloudier look. The sponge prints may be delicate or heavy depending on the pressure applied, dense or widely spaced, according to taste. They may be close- or open-grained; one side of a marine sponge is finer-textured than the other. For subtle variation, apply glaze of one colour to the surface, coat the sponge with another and smudge it gently into the wet glaze. Sponging is an attractive finish for walls and furniture, but can look messy on skirting boards (baseboards), architraves and other moulded surfaces.

Use a marine sponge if possible. Suppliers of specialist brushes also sell unbleached sponges, which are far cheaper than those sold by chemists (pharmacists). Rinse the sponge out in water to soften it, but squeeze it well and let it dry out slightly before use.

Sponging may be easy, but to be successful, it needs a delicate touch. Too much glaze on the sponge produces thick, coagulated colour and irritating repetitions of patterns. There are two ways to avoid this. After dipping the sponge into the glaze – using a paint tray as a container – dab it lightly over a piece of lining paper to

Sponging

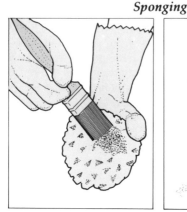

1 *Painting glaze on to sponge gives more control.*

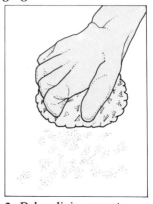

2 *Dab on lining paper to remove excess.*

Sponge the second colour lightly over the first, changing direction regularly to avoid repetitive patterns.

remove the excess glaze, before you embark on the wall. Alternatively, paint the glaze on to the sponge with a brush. It is time-consuming, but gives more control.

Corners and irregular surfaces – like radiators – can be awkward. Thick bands of glaze build up as you try to manoeuvre the sponge into tight angles, smearing the section you have just done. Approach these areas with caution, and a virtually dry sponge. If necessary, nudge any excess glaze into corners with a stippling brush.

As you dab away, keep changing the position of the sponge to avoid making too regular a pattern. Inadvertent print-repeats strike a monotonous note in what should be a random harmony. Repeated pattern can be beautiful, but it needs to be controlled and skilfully applied.

When working over a larger area your sponge will become clogged with glaze and the pattern more rigid. Rinse the sponge out regularly in white spirit or water as appropriate, but squeeze it out thoroughly. Any white spirit left in the sponge will open up the glaze (as in sponging off).

Stippling

Speckled, freckled and dappled are all words that have been used to describe the impression that stippling gives. Stippled surfaces have a shimmering quality, an illusion created by countless tiny flecks of colour made as the glaze is distressed to expose the base coat beneath. The base coat should be several tones lighter than the glaze to get the full benefit of the technique, or be an entirely different colour.

The texture of the finish varies according to the brush you use. The traditional stippling brush produces a very subtle effect, best suited to furniture or small rooms. It can disappear altogether at a distance. You can use any flat brush for stippling: specialist stippling brushes, made of fine bristle, are very expensive. The rubber variety, though cheaper, soon perishes when used with white spirit. A long-haired paint roller produces an attractive approximation of the traditional brush-stipple.

Lay on the glaze as evenly as you can, using an ordinary decorator's brush. On walls, paint a strip at a time, from ceiling to floor, about 600mm (2ft) wide. Dab the glaze with the brush, keeping your movements firm and regular; if you pat too hard, the brush will slide, leaving skid marks. Stipple over the entire section, to within 50mm (2in.) of the edge, paint the next strip and

A stippling brush is used to smooth out brushmarks in the glaze, leaving a soft haze of flecked colour.

Stippling

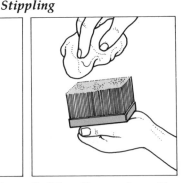

1 Prime brush with a little
glaze before you start.

2 Wipe off excess glaze with a
rag to prevent colour build up.

stipple over the join to blend the two together. Work fast
to keep each edge wet for long enough to merge evenly
into the next. If the glaze becomes tacky, blending is
impossible, leaving you with heavy streaks of colour.
(This can happen with any technique where glaze is laid
on in sections.) If this does happen, wipe the glaze off the
whole section and start again.

When you begin, the clean brush may remove too
much glaze. If so, grease the bristles lightly with a little
glaze to prime them. As you work, wipe the brush
frequently with a lint-free cotton rag to remove the
excess. Uneven patches can be touched up later by
stippling on a little more colour, rather than stippling it
off.

This technique is particularly effective on mouldings
such as those around door panels, on cornices and
picture-rails. Add a touch of refinement by removing
the stippled glaze from raised surfaces, emphasizing the
highlights as the glaze remains in the recesses like a
tinted shadow. Leave the glaze for about 30 minutes until
tacky, and then run a finger – wrapped in mutton-cloth
(cheese cloth) moistened with white spirit – over the
most prominent surfaces.

Stippling is frequently used for blending colour, in
marbling or as a decorative effect on walls and furniture.
Different colours or tones of the same colour, are laid on
in bands, streaks or patches, and stippled together to
achieve soft gradations of shade. In this way, you can, for
example, lower a high ceiling in a small room by shading
the wall upwards from light to dark.

Dragging and combing

These rudimentary woodgraining techniques are among the most sophisticated of decorative treatments. Dragging in particular, if skilfully done, has the elegance of a fine raw silk. A word of warning: dragging will accentuate any irregularities in walls or woodwork.

The same method is used for both dragging and combing. A brush or comb is pulled through the glaze, leaving a series of parallel lines of varying width and delicacy. Traditionally 'floggers' and 'dragging' brushes are used, but an emulsion brush or jamb duster will do. Woodgraining combs come in different sizes and gradations. You can use a wide-toothed hair comb instead, or make your own from cardboard or linoleum.

Dragging a wall can be done by one person, but it is far simpler with two. One applies the glaze in 600mm (2ft) wide strips, the other drags from ceiling to floor, ideally in one movement. Start at a corner and if necessary, use a plumbline suspended from the ceiling to get your first line perfectly vertical. Place the bristles of the brush lightly at the point where the wall and ceiling meet. With your arm at an angle of about 30°, relax and pull the brush downwards through the glaze, through to the floor. Lessen the pressure on the brush and gently lift the bristles off the wall as you reach the end of the stroke.

You may find it impossible to keep a straight line, especially if you are coming down a ladder. Bring the first stroke down as far as you can without wobbling, pref-

Dragging and combing

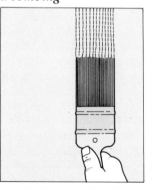

A wide-toothed comb or a brush is pulled through glaze, leaving a series of parallel lines.

erably below eye level. Then start from the bottom, dragging upwards to meet the first stroke, overlap slightly and lift the brush off. The long flexible bristles of a flogger make this feat relatively simple. Make successive joins at different levels, so that they will be less conspicuous.

Dragging should always follow the grain on woodwork. On panels and mouldings, drag away from corners to prevent pools of glaze from collecting. The sequence on doors should be panels, muntin (the central upright), crossrails and stiles. Any mouldings are best completed first and left to dry.

Combing can look rather stiff on woodwork, but is very dramatic on floors. With both combing and dragging, do not limit yourself to straight vertical lines. Try cross-hatching, and curving lines for a less traditional but nonetheless attractive finish.

Dragged mouldings – drag away from the corners – add distinction to the dullest door.

Ragging and rag-rolling

Appropriately enough, ragged finishes usually conjure up images of textiles – watered silk, crushed velvet, or crumpled cotton. In texture ragged finishes are as different from each other as fabrics are. You can use anything which is reasonably absorbent, lint-free and colour-fast when used with solvents. Newspaper qualifies as rag in this context. You can use your rag as a soft pad – one piece wrapped inside another – to blot the glaze into a hazy cloud of colour, or keep it firmly crumpled in your hand as you crease and crimp the glaze into a more distinctive pattern. Ragging looks most effective on large areas like walls and ceilings. On furniture it can seem coarse and too overwhelming for such constricted dimensions.

Apply the glaze in a similar way to stippling, but work as evenly as you can with wider strips of colour – about 1m (1yd). For the perfect ragged finish, the glaze should be stippled or sponged before ragging, to obliterate all brush-marks. You really need two people for this.

Pat your rag over the glaze, changing direction as you move, and rearranging the folds in the cloth to avoid monotonous prints. Change the rags as they become soaked with glaze, laying them flat to dry before discarding (see p. 45).

Rag-rolling produces a more uniform pattern. Take a piece of cloth – about 200mm × 200mm (8in. × 8in.) – and roll it into a cigar shape. Holding both ends, lay it flat against the surface and roll it firmly through the glaze, working (on walls) from the bottom upwards. Repeat the process, slightly overlapping the prints.

Ragging and rag-rolling

1 *In ragging, pat rag over glaze with one hand.*

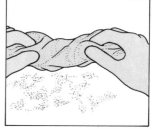

2 *Use both hands for rolling; the pattern is more uniform.*

Spattering

Used on its own, with one colour or several, or combined with other techniques, spattering is charming. Use a fairly thin glaze and a thick brush to hold more colour. You will also need a second brush or strip of wood.

Tap your glaze-laden brush hard against the other, while holding both over the surface. Droplets of colour will spatter across it. A finer spatter can be achieved by dipping a round fitch or artist's brush in thinned glaze, holding it over the surface with one hand and 'tickling' the bristles with the forefinger of the other.

Spattering

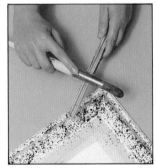

1 Tap the brush hard to produce a bold spatter.

2 Flick the bristles for a fine speckle of colour.

Postscript

There are several points to remember:

1 Always wipe smudged glaze off unfinished areas before it hardens. When dry, these patches will show up under subsequent coats of glaze.

2 Never leave crumpled glaze and spirit-soaked rags lying around as they are liable to ignite spontaneously. Dry them flat before disposal, or put them in a covered tin.

3 With most techniques you will need to touch up the ceiling after you have decorated the walls.

4 Allow each glaze coat to dry overnight before applying another.

5 If an effect seems too stark on your practice board, try it over a base coat of the same colour, but a lighter tone; or put another glaze on top to soften the entire finish.

Marbling

Real marbles are the product of violent, creative disturbances in the earth's crust thousands of years ago. Molten limestone, fused with mineral deposits, cooled and then crystallized into an infinite variety of forms. Inspired by nature's inventiveness, artists have developed techniques both to imitate marble, and to produce imaginative variations of their own. Much contemporary marbling is stylized, the colours and forms only distantly related to the real thing. Marble is worth examining when you come across a piece. It will serve both as a model and a spur to your imagination. There is no limit to the colours you can use for fantasy marble, but the best results are usually achieved when using colours from the same range – warm reds, browns and yellows, or cool blues and greens. In real marble the stark colour contrasts are usually provided by the veins.

Numerous marbling techniques have been developed, using both water and oil colours, but you can also get breathtaking results with very basic methods. Adapt these to suit your purpose as practice improves skill. The ground should be well prepared, and finished with an undercoat and two coats of white eggshell. Marbling is suitable on walls and woodwork provided they are completely smooth. Be subtle about marbling over large areas; the effect can be overwhelming in such quantity. Although many purists condemn marbling on doors and skirting (baseboards) as being unrealistic, it can look both rich and impressive.

'Rubbing-in'

'Rubbing-in' is the term given to laying on the coloured glaze. Two methods are described here; experiment with both to see which you find best. Decide on the basic colours of your marble. Two will suffice for your first attempt. Raw sienna/cerulean blue and raw sienna/white are used here, as examples.

Make up two batches of tinted glaze (see pp. 34-6), diluted with white spirit (paint thinner). Work a section at a time, in panels of about 300mm × 300mm (12in. × 12in.), depending on the overall area. Dab streaks and blotches of raw sienna/cerulean blue on to the surface, using a 25-50mm (1-2in.) decorator's (paint) brush or a fitch, and leave spaces between. Try to get movement

A marble finish applied to contemporary furnishings complements the real marble of the fireplace.

and common direction into your shapes; colours in natural marble are fluid. Using a second brush, fill in the spaces with raw sienna/white, leaving a little of the background still uncovered. Then stipple the rivulets of colour together with a brush or sponge, being selective as you want to keep each colour still partially distinct. With a badger or hogshair softener blend the colours together. The brush should be held lightly, at right angles to the surface, and swung gently in all directions. Just the tips of the bristles should touch the glaze. The colours blur and soften, taking on depth and vibrancy, like stone under water. Rag over the surface with paper or cotton to break up the glaze and soften once more.

In the second method a transparent glaze – of commercial oil glaze and white spirit – is brushed over the surface. The consistency must be very thin. Dissolve small quantities of pigment with white spirit – old saucers are useful here – and then float the colours on to the glaze, using a mop or brush to create streaks and pools of colour as before. The surface is then softened, ragged and softened again. This method gives greater translucency than the first, which some may prefer.

Veining

A goose feather is the marbler's traditional veining tool. It is strong and versatile. Used sideways on, or tip only, it produces fine lines. The vane or barbs of the feather can be divided into a series of delicate points – like parallel nibs – and drawn sideways through the glaze for a striated or slightly ridged effect. Dip the feather first in water, then in white spirit, and part the vane to form clumps.

A swordliner, used by signwriters, serves as a substitute but is less versatile. Artist's brushes, lining fitches, oil and wax crayons, and conte pencils are all used in marbling, each giving a different emphasis of line.

Dip the tip of the quill or brush into your veining pigment. This should be either a darker tone of the background or a contrasting colour. Holding the quill or brush between finger and thumb, drag it across the surface, twirling it lightly from side to side, changing the pressure and direction for greater variation. Follow the characteristics of marble. Veins are angular rather than undulating, and even curves are made up of tiny straight lines. Think of veins as crystalline rivers with their many tributaries, diverging and joining, but with purpose and

Rubbing-in and veining

1 Randomly lay on two colours of glaze with brush.

2 Stipple selectively with another brush to blend colour.

3 Blur colour by lightly brushing with softener.

4 Use crumpled paper or cloth to rag the glaze surface.

5 Vein the surface with a darker or contrasting colour by twirling and dragging a goose feather over the glazes.

direction. Beware of being too erratic and of drawing in too many. Blend the veins into the background, using a badger or hogshair softener.

For further variation, dip the quill tip first into one colour, then another. Alternatively, follow the first vein – running parallel, then crossing and re-crossing – with another quill dipped in the second colour. Use the goose feather sideways on to create parallel runnels of colour, twisting and turning to form a web of lines, much like foam on a dying wave. Add a second glaze when the first has dried, and run new colour along the veins, creating the illusion of great depth as one layer builds up upon another.

Special effects

All the impurities and blemishes which appear in real marble can be recreated by simple techniques. Spattering (see p. 45), with thinned colour or white spirit, which will break up the glaze, enlivens a dull marble, and stippling (see pp. 40-1) with a round fitch adds variation to the texture.

Create dramatic fissures by slapping the glaze with a loosely held rag. Clingfilm (plastic wrap), pressed lightly against the surface, will lift off the glaze in irregular patterns very similar to those found in genuine marble.

Copying nature

These techniques are used, together or separately, to imitate natural marble.

White marble is one of the simplest to imitate. Lay a very thin glaze, tinted with white, over the surface. Make up two pale tones using white, raw umber and a little black. Add a touch of yellow ochre to one to give warmth. Float them into the glaze, very sparingly, and soften. The veins are of darker grey, made of black and white with a hint of ultramarine blue, forming quite straight, branching lines.

Sienna marble includes many variations on a yellow theme, ranging from a deep ochre to burnt sienna. Float patches of raw sienna into the glaze, interspersed with ochre and burnt sienna. After softening, open the glaze again in places, using a brush or sponge dipped in white spirit to reveal the ground coat. Rag gently and soften once more. Use ivory black and burnt umber for the veins, creating a network of uneven, angular spots of colour. Put in the occasional white vein – thin streaks made with a feather dipped in white spirit and white pigment.

Black and green marble is worked over a black base coat. Lay a very thin glaze of green, made of Prussian blue and raw sienna, and rag it to open up the base coat. Veinings are put in using white and a lighter green, made from Prussian blue and a chrome or cadmium yellow. Spatter with the original green and draw in very fine white veins across broken areas of black ground. Very little softening is needed.

Exotic effects

Some of the more elaborate finishes require a lot of practice to do well, but the brief guidelines given here may encourage you to experiment. These finishes are best suited to small items, likes boxes, lamps and furniture.

Malachite has a base of emerald or 'tourmaline' eggshell paint. A thick glaze of viridian is dabbed over the surface, varying the tone by mixing it with a little raw umber, Prussian blue and a faint hint of yellow ochre. After ragging and softening, the frilled rings, characteristic of malachite, are drawn in with a piece of cardboard torn along a folded edge. Then use a round fitch to make small whorls in the areas between, adding a light stipple here and there to blur hard edges.

Malachite effects

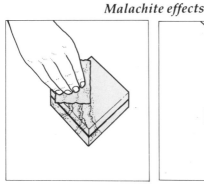

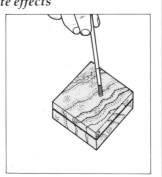

1 Draw in frilled rings with a piece of cardboard.

2 Use a round fitch for small whorls between them.

Lapis lazuli is imitated with swathes of French ultra-marine and Prussian blue glaze, spread over a white ground. Cloudy streaks of white, shaded with raw umber, are stippled on. The overall effect is of the sky at night. After ragging and softening, spatters of Prussian, pale blue (made from white and ultramarine) and white are added. Dip a dry brush into bronze powder and tap it lightly into the glaze, like fine drifts and speckles of gold.

Lapis lazuli

1 Rag the base coats to soften colour.

2 Tap bronze powder lightly into glaze.

A picture frame with a lapis lazuli finish.

Tortoiseshell on transfer metal background and a malachite-finished box.

Tortoiseshell requires a pale gold or custard yellow base coat. A fairly thick glaze, tinted with raw sienna, is spread over it in diagonal streaks. Denser blobs and streaks of raw sienna are added, using pigment and a little white spirit. Burnt umber is applied in the same way, with a finer brush and the whole surface is softened. A few spatters and further blobs of burnt umber and a final softening gives greater depth and variation.

Transfer metal makes a beautiful background for lapis lazuli and tortoiseshell. It takes practice to apply well. First seal the surface with shellac, allow to dry, and then brush it over thinly with gold size. Leave it for 30 minutes, or until just tacky (follow the manufacturer's instructions). Take a sheet of the metal leaf, still attached to tissue paper, and press it – metal-side down – on to the surface. Rub firmly with your fingers and peel away the paper. Cover the whole area with metal leaf, and then dust off loose particles with a dry artist's brush. Leave it to dry completely overnight, and then polish gently with a pad of cotton wool. Seal the surface with another coat of shellac before applying the glaze. Use Dutch metal for a cheap imitation of gold.

Woodgraining

Straight grain and heartgrain are the basic motifs of the woodgrainer's craft. There are as many pattern variations for each as there are types of wood.

If a tree is split vertically, the heart-wood is revealed as a succession of concentric, elliptical rings, running down the length of the trunk. They spread outwards from the centre, giving way gradually to the tramline pattern of the outer, straight grain.

The techniques for reproducing the pattern of straight and heart grain are described here in relation to oak. They may be used, with slight modifications of colour and texture, to make attractive imitations of ash and pine. Few woodgrainers try to copy natural wood exactly. The overall impression is more important than total accuracy.

Graining colours

Conventionally, graining is worked over a coloured ground, appropriate to the individual wood. White eggshell paint provides the best surface to work on, tinted with yellow ochre for pine, or with ochre and raw umber for oak and ash. Weathered oak has a grey ground, mixed from white and black.

Oil glaze must be used very thinly to avoid ridges forming as graining tools are dragged through it. Commercial glaze has too much body to be really successful. Make up a glaze of 60% boiled linseed oil to 40% white spirit (paint thinner), with the sparing addition of 'driers' (drying agents for oil paints, which can be bought from artist's suppliers). This can then be tinted with artist's oils, dissolved in white spirit. Some specialist shops also sell the traditional 'scumble' glaze, which is pre-tinted in common graining colours. This is thinned with white spirit.

Equal quantities of water and vinegar, tinted with powdered pigment, make a delicate and quick-drying graining colour. If you are graining larger areas, like a door, you will need an assistant to lay on the colour while you work swiftly before the glaze dries. This technique does require a badger softener rather than the hogshair variety. Badger softeners are expensive, but the small sizes will be adequate for beginners' needs.

Left: *Woodgraining conventionally, as here, simulates the colours of natural woods. An overall impression of the wood, rather than an exact copy, is what you are trying to achieve.*

This is an exception to the general rule that washes should be laid over water-based grounds. Water-colour does not form an even film over oil paint, tending to separate into droplets – a phenomenon known as 'cissing'. Rub the surface with a damp sponge, dipped in whiting (powdered chalk) and brush off any excess. This leaves the surface free of grease, allowing the graining colour to adhere properly.

If you are attempting to reproduce the real thing, here are a few colour guidelines for the commoner woods:

Ash and oak   white, raw sienna, raw umber and a little black; add a touch of burnt sienna or Venetian red for dark oak

Weathered oak   black, burnt umber and ultramarine blue

Pine   raw umber, burnt sienna and a touch of black

Try out less naturalistic colour combinations as well – for example, grey or soft blue over white, or a white glaze grained over a crimson ground. These fantasy timbers can be more successful in the end than a poor copy of genuine wood.

Straight grain

Try out different brushes to vary the density and texture of the straight grain, as occurs in natural wood. Floggers, dragging brushes, jamb dusters, steel and rubber combs are all used, depending on the effect required.

Lay on the glaze with a decorator's (painter's) brush, and paint in an irregular panel of darker tone – uniformity always looks artificial. Drag through the glaze from top to bottom, jogging the brush occasionally to imitate the unevenness of true woodgrain. Use a selection of combs and brushes on the same panel for different densities of grain. For still further interest, use a fine steel comb to drag a second set of lines, at a slight diagonal, over the first, in one or two sections only.

The pores of oak wood are put in with a flogger at this stage, and the reason for the name of this brush becomes apparent. Starting at the bottom of your panel, hold the flogger almost horizontal over the surface and tap the glaze very lightly with the bristle tips, 'flogging' upwards in vertical lines. The dragged lines are scored with tiny marks, making the painted grain look convincingly real. If the glaze is left to dry slightly before flogging, finer marks are produced. Alternatively, you can use a badger softener, to imitate the close-grained woods.

To obtain a natural-looking straight grain finish, first lay on glaze with a brush then drag through with a selection of combs.

Heartgrain

There are different techniques for producing heartgrain patterns. These can be painted on with a fine artist's brush, or the glaze can be removed with the edge of a comb, wrapped in cloth. A rubber graining tool, which can be obtained from specialist shops, is perhaps the most fun to use. This is dragged downwards through the glaze, moving the curved head backwards and forwards in a smooth, rocking motion. The quicker you rock, the denser the pattern. These graining tools work well for oak and pine, but produce too regular a pattern to imitate the distortions found in other heartwoods. If the effect is too hard, soften slightly with a hogshair or badger softener. Your dragged lines should curve slightly

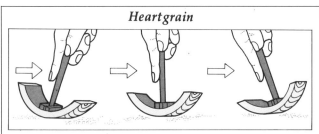

Heartgrain

Drag the graining tool through the glaze, rocking the curved head backwards and forwards.

The graining tool will effectively reproduce oak and pine wood patterns though they are too regular for some woods.

around the heartgrain, merging into straight grain once more on either side.

Allow the panel to dry and go over it again with a thin glaze, tinted as before, dragged and flogged over the heartgrain. Darker tones can be stippled into areas of the glaze before dragging, for greater depth and realism.

Knots

Dip a cork or round fitch in a colour appropriate to the wood – a darker tone of the glaze colours. Press it vertically into the glaze and twirl it on the spot. Draw in a few small cracks, radiating out from the centre, using the handle of a fine artist's brush to remove the glaze. Soften slightly.

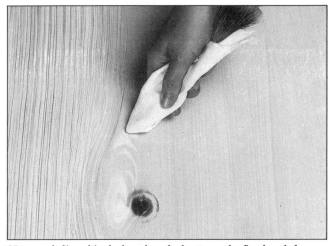

Use a cork dipped in darker glaze for knots, and a fine brush for cracks. Wrap brush handle in rag to remove areas of glaze.

Decorative woods

The techniques already described can be adapted slightly to produce simplified versions of decorative woods like mahogany and bird's eye maple. For sophisticated representations, further refinements of technique would be necessary, but exciting results can be achieved with a modicum of skill.

Mahogany

Mahogany, with its rich warm tones, was a mainstay of Victorian interiors. You might choose, for example, to turn your bath into a period piece with mahogany panelled sides. Tint the base coat of white eggshell with Venetian red, yellow ochre and white, and glaze with burnt sienna and Vandyke brown. Follow instructions for the straight grain as described on p. 57.

Lay on glaze; make central streak a darker tone.

Draw a dry brush through glaze to make heartgrain pattern.

*Soften with a badger softener, then cover with thin darker glaze.
'Mottle' the surface, removing narrow bands for highlights.*

Lay on the glaze, making a central streak of darker tone, tinted with raw umber. Use a dry decorator's brush – 25mm (1in.) or slightly wider – to make the heartgrain pattern. Start just left of centre, at the bottom of the panel. With the tip parallel to the vertical edge, draw the brush upwards through the glaze for about 100mm (4in.). Curve it round to the right and down again, straightening the brush as you do so. Repeat the stroke, building up a series of ellipses to create a rough oval, flattened on the left side. Soften gently, upwards towards the top of the curve. Straight grain should also be softened, but diagonally. When dry, go over it with a thin glaze of Vandyke brown and burnt umber. 'Mottle' the surface – removing narrow bands of glaze to make highlights – using a professional 'mottler' or a small dragging brush. Soften slightly and flog with a badger softener.

Bird's eye maple

Bird's eye maple adds a decorative flourish to small pieces of furniture, panels and frames. The base coat is tinted with yellow ochre, the graining colour with raw sienna and burnt umber. With a 50mm (2in.) dry brush, drag downwards through the glaze – shifting pressure and direction, stopping and starting – to produce a creased ribbon of colour. Cover the whole surface with these vertical bands, overlapping them slightly. Dab the knuckle of your small finger sharply into the glaze to form dots for the 'eyes' of the maple. Allow to dry for about 15 minutes (if using oil glaze), and then soften slightly. The graining can be done with crayon – in a tone close to burnt sienna – while the glaze is still wet. Heart and straight grain meander around the dots, much like contour lines on a map.

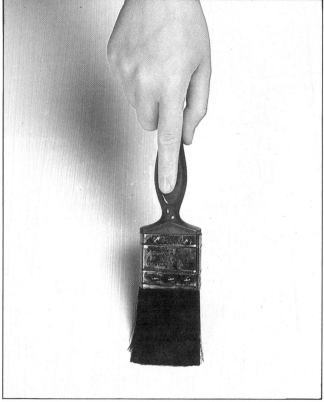

Drag a dry brush through glaze to create creased ribbon effect.

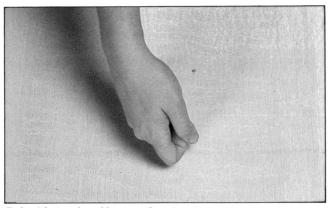

Dab with your knuckle to produce 'eyes'.

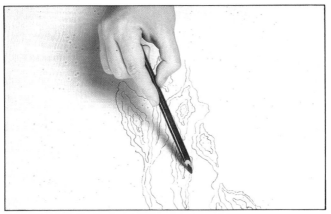

Draw in graining with a crayon or a fine artist's brush while the glaze is still wet.

Painting sequence for doors

Woodgraining is used most frequently as a decorative treatment for doors. The sequence for painting is the same as that for dragging (see pp. 42-3): mouldings, panels, muntin, cross-rails and stiles. For beginners it can be very hard to do the whole door in one continuous process, without marking areas just painted. Cheat by doing it in stages, using tape to mask off sections before graining, and letting each dry before starting on the next. This is laborious, so consider using water-colour which will dry much faster. The whole door can be grained and varnished in one day, rubbed down with whiting, overgrained and varnished again on the following day.

Stencilling

Patterned fabrics are a useful source of ideas for stencils. The palm-leaf was inspired by one motif in a complex design.

Repeating pattern by the simple means of stencilling may seem mechanical, but the results have a spontaneity and charm, which no other form of decorative painting quite matches. The design can be as simple as a spray of flowers, or an interpretation of a Gauguin painting.

Before starting a stencilling scheme, it is worth taking precise measurements of the room or piece of furniture you intend to decorate. Spaces between pattern repeats can be juggled to fit – perfect symmetry is not essential – but good measurements and some careful calculations can prevent disasters.

Designing stencils

There are numerous ready-made stencils available from artist's suppliers and specialist shops. Many are based on traditional designs taken from sources as diverse as Pharaonic Egypt and early American folk art. If you choose to make your own, you can copy designs from old fabrics and wallpapers, tiles and pottery.

If the pattern is already the size you want, simply trace it out on to tracing paper. It is quite easy to enlarge or reduce a pattern. Trace the pattern, and then enclose it in a rectangle or square. Divide this up into squares of equal size, by drawing a grid of vertical and horizontal lines. On a separate sheet of tracing paper draw another grid, increasing or reducing the size of the squares as required. Then copy the pattern on to the second grid, using the squares as a guideline.

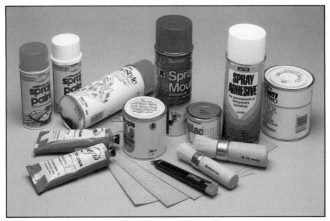

Cut out your own designs using stencil paper, and experiment with traditional brushes and oils, or with spray paints.

Transferring the design

The design must now be transferred on to stencil card. Sheets of acetate are transparent and convenient for positioning, especially if your design is made up of more than one stencil. Acetate, however, splits quite easily with intricate work, and is too flimsy for large patterns. Oiled stencil card can be used instead.

Tape the tracing paper on to the card, with a sheet of carbon paper between and go over the pattern with a hard point such as a knitting needle or ballpoint pen. Alternatively, rub a soft pencil over the back of the design and proceed as before, without the carbon.

For a multi-coloured design you will need a stencil for each colour, unless you want them to merge, as in shadowing. Transfer the relevant sections on to separate sheets of stencil card.

Cutting stencils

Place the stencil paper on a piece of glass or cutting mat. Using a craft knife or scalpel, cut round the outline of the drawing. Keep the blade at a 45° angle; this gives the stencil a bevelled edge which helps to prevent paint seeping under it. If you gently manoeuvre the blade from side to side as you cut, a faintly wavy edge is formed, making the outline less hard. Holding the blade at an angle also makes it easier to negotiate curves.

Always cut away from sharp corners rather than into them, in case you overshoot the mark. If you do make a mistake, you can mend the stencil by sticking masking tape over the cut, back and front. Over small areas this is as good as having a new stencil card – and far less laborious.

It is very important to make clean cuts in the stencil, for any furry edges will show up badly when stencilling is complete. If the blade breaks, it is easy and inexpensive to replace, but use a pair of pliers to do so – it is even easier to cut your fingers.

If using two or more colours, first cut out separate stencils for the different sections, align them correctly and then cut through all the thicknesses to square up the sheets. Make small holes or notches near each edge – again through all the stencils. When you fix each stencil, you can make light pencil marks through the holes to help with lining up.

Stencilling in two colours

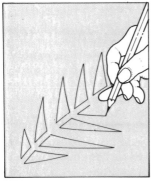

1 Draw or trace design on to paper.

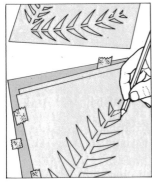

2 Select colours for each part of design.

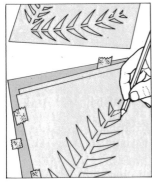

3 Transfer design to stencil cards – one for each colour.

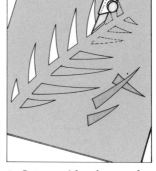

4 Cut out with a sharp craft knife.

5 Check pattern cards align; match corners.

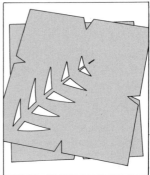

6 Cut each side of each card to ensure alignment.

Fixing the stencil

Before committing yourself, try out your stencil on eggshell-covered hardboard, to experiment with colours and densities. You can fix the stencil to the surface with masking tape but there can be problems in getting the stencil to lie flat. One solution is to use a spray adhesive, sold in aerosols as re-positioning glues for graphic design work. Spray the back of the stencil lightly and allow the solution to evaporate briefly. When the stencil is only just still tacky, it can be pressed on to the surface, and will adhere without leaving a deposit – or taking off the base coat colour when you remove it. This precaution also prevents paint from seeping under the stencil.

Pigments for stencilling

Pigments of all kinds can be used for stencilling, but they should be fast-drying – especially if you are using different colours. Acrylics are favoured by many stencil-lers, thinned with water and a little PVA (yellow) glue to assist adhesion. Signwriter's colours and japan colours (familiar in the US and now sold in a few specialist shops in Britain) are particularly good. Artist's oils are slow to dry and tend to smudge easily, but work quite well if mixed with white oil-based undercoat. Car spray is another possibility, but make sure the room is well-ventilated and always wear a mask.

Brushes for stencilling are traditionally short and stubby – professional brushes are widely available, but round fitches and artist's brushes can be used as well. Small pieces of synthetic or marine sponge make an attractive alternative.

Choice of colours will obviously depend on your décor, but a couple of points are worth mentioning. Changing the weight of colours – the degree of light or dark tone if represented in black and white – will alter your design. Intricate details stencilled in a pale green might vanish altogether in conjunction with a strong red. Soft, older colours are particularly suited to stencilling. If you find your colours too bright, tone them down with a touch of their complementary colour, or some raw umber.

More than one stencil may be used to make up a complete design. Registration marks are cut at the stencil edge, and the first colour allowed to dry before applying the next.

Application

The colour is applied with the brush or sponge almost dry. The pigment should be dissolved in the appropriate solvent in a small, shallow container. Dip in the brush and dab off most of the colour on to a spare piece of paper before you begin. Work from the edge of the cut-out, easing off towards the centre – using a firm tapping or 'pouncing' movement. Allow the colour to dry for about 30 seconds, before moving the stencil on to the next section. Wipe the stencil clean with rags and solvent as the paint builds up. When using an aerosol, shake the can well, hold it about 150mm (6in.) away from the surface and spray very lightly. Never use it on an oil ground as it would dissolve the paint.

Metallic powders can be used in stencilling to create

Registration of the design

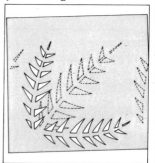

1 *Cut an acetate stencil for each colour area. Each stencil should include keylines for the intended patten repeats.*

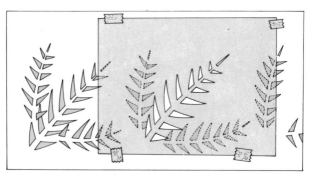

2 *These keylines enable you to register accurately the separate areas of the design.*

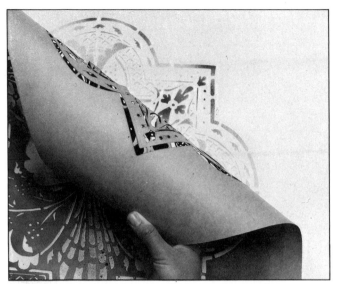

Spray the colour through and gently remove the stencil.

most exotic effects, especially over a background of black or red. Use quick-drying gold size as an adhesive, painted through the stencil, and tinted with a little oil colour so that you can see areas you may have missed. Allow to dry for 30 minutes until just tacky, and then dab on the powder with a brush. Leave it to dry, then rub off any surplus with a cotton pad.

Always protect your stencilling with a coat of varnish. You will need to cover the entire surface – this applies to walls as well – not just the stencilled area.

Care of stencils

It is worth taking care of your stencils; you may want to use them again, for repair jobs, or another area entirely.

Stencils will last longer if you brush on a coating of french polish or shellac, which both protects the surface, and makes it easier to wipe off surplus paint while in use. Wipe the stencil clean when you have finished, and store it flat. If you have used spray mount, the stencils will tend to be tacky so sprinkle with talcum powder before storing.

For large scale jobs, when a stencil is used repeatedly, it is wise to have a spare copy. This must be an exact replica of the first. Spray through the first stencil with car spray on to another sheet of stencil board and cut out as before.

Varnishing

Most decorative paint finishes will require a protective coat of varnish. The exceptions are areas which are unlikely to suffer much wear and tear – notably walls finished with a reasonably durable combination of oil glaze and oil-based paint.

Types of varnish

Oil- and alkyd-based varnishes are traditionally used in decorative painting. They give added depth to the colours, are quick-drying and hard. As with all products which contain oils, there is a danger of yellowing with age. This can be made less noticeable by tinting the varnish with white eggshell or artist's oil paint, but some clarity will be lost. Layers of varnish tinted with artist's oils give extraordinary richness to a surface. Varnishes range in colour from very pale to a deep, tawny hue. Use the palest form for light paintwork. They are sold in matt, eggshell or full gloss finishes, with the old-fashioned 'carriage varnish' providing the most brilliant sheen.

Polyurethane varnishes, made of synthetic resins, have attained some popularity because of their extreme toughness. This unyielding quality can be a disadvantage if any moisture is trapped under the film, as it will eventually lead to chipping. In contrast, oil-based varnishes allow the paint to breathe, and moisture to escape. If badly applied, polyurethanes can give an object the appearance of cheap plastic. Opinions differ considerably, but it would be advisable to use oil- and alkyd-based varnishes for most jobs, keeping the polyurethanes for floors, fireplaces and other areas which need an impenetrable finish. Polyurethanes come in matt, eggshell and gloss finishes, and some are available in aerosol cans.

Emulsion varnishes are used principally over wallpapers to give them a washable finish. Made of PVA or acrylic, they are water-soluble and useful for protecting washes and emulsion (latex) finishes, and flat-oil paint. Oil- and alkyd-based varnishes can also be used over water-based paints. Emulsion varnish should only be used to protect an oil glaze coat if this has thoroughly hardened.

French polish is a form of shellac, which is made from

insect secretions gathered from certain trees, mainly in India. It can be used over paint to give a particularly fine finish to small decorative items, including boxes and frames.

Nitro-cellulose lacquers should be used over car spray paints, but never over oil-based paints.

Brushes

Ordinary decorator's brushes may be used, or the traditional oval varnish brushes. Always keep a separate set of brushes for varnishing, and make sure they are thoroughly clean. Another brush will be needed if you are using shellac.

Matt varnish may be used on walls for a uniform finish.

Preparation

Successful varnishing depends as much on working conditions as it does on application. The surface you are working on, the atmosphere, and the object you are varnishing should all be as free of dust as possible.

Stir the varnish well according to the manufacturer's instructions and strain it through a pair of old nylon tights into another container, to remove any grit. Wipe over the object with a tack rag before you begin.

Pour a little varnish into a separate container, dip in your brush, and then work the varnish into the bristles by brushing them out firmly on a clean surface, like a piece of hardboard (masonite). This prevents the varnish from frothing.

The varnish should stand at room temperature for at least a day; alternatively, you can place the tin in luke-warm water to bring it up to the right temperature. If it still does not flow smoothly, add a little white spirit (paint thinner), in the proportion of about 1 part solvent to 3 parts varnish.

Varnishing the surface

Do not overload your brush – no more than 15mm (½in.) of the bristles should be covered. Press the bristles against the inside of the pot rather than scraping against the rim. This prevents bubbles forming on the surface of the varnish, which would show up on the finished piece.

Lay on the varnish with the grain on wood, vertically on walls. Cross-brush and lay off with the grain, or towards the light, as appropriate to the surface. It is very important to keep the wet edge going as you work, blending each section into the next as you would when painting with eggshell. The varnish should flow, so do not overwork it, nor brush it in as you would with paint.

One problem in varnishing is that it is very easy to miss sections, so it is always necessary to check the area you are covering from an angle. Sections you have over-looked will always show up.

Matt finish

Interior woodwork like doors, architraves, skirting boards (baseboards) and fire surrounds are difficult to bring up to a perfectly smooth finish. A matt varnish will not show up surface flaws to the same extent as eggshell or gloss. Any imperfections can be further disguised by creating a slightly textured surface, laying on the varnish, then stippling it out with a brush. This has two advantages. There is less danger of drips forming, and of the varnish building up in mouldings and corners. The varnish also forms a strong bond with the coat below.

Satin finish

For a finer finish on doors, fire surrounds and furniture, use an eggshell varnish. When the first coat is dry, rub it down carefully with a grade 1000 or 1200 wet and dry paper. Wet the surface first. Be particularly careful on the first coat since there is always a danger of rubbing through and damaging the paint below. To be absolutely safe, apply a second coat of varnish before doing any rubbing. Wipe the surface with a damp cloth and let it dry. Make a large wad of steel wool, using the finest grade 0000, dip it into furniture wax polish, and rub the surface in one direction, following the grain of the wood. The surface will develop a soft sheen and when the wax is dry, buff it up with a soft duster. Polish it again at intervals with wax and a soft cloth.

Fine finishes

For small attractive pieces you may want an even finer finish. This is done by building up the layers of varnish – a minimum of three is required. For the toughest finish, with the most depth, use a gloss varnish. (Even if you prefer a satin finish, build up the first layers with gloss and finish off with eggshell varnish.) Rub down between each coat with grade 1000 or 1200 wet and dry paper. When the final coat has been smoothed down, go over it again with an abrasive paste – a proprietary burnishing cream, brass polish or T-Cut (car polish). Rottenstone, a very fine abrasive powder, is used by professionals – rubbed on with a cloth lubricated with oil. Finally, for the smoothest finish of all, rub the surface with ordinary household flour. Finish off with wax furniture polish.

Small decorative items, like boxes and occasional tables, could be french polished after varnishing. This is a laborious process beyond the scope of this book to describe, and involves building up layers of shellac with a 'rubber' of cotton wool soaked in polish and wrapped in fine cotton. It is painstaking, but will give your masterpiece an elegance which no other finish equals.

Acknowledgements

Swallow Books gratefully acknowledge the assistance given to them in the production of *Decorative Paint Finishes* by the following people and organizations. We apologize to anyone we may have omitted to mention.

Photographs: Reproduced by permission of The American Museum in Britain, Bath 4; Jon Bouchier 6, 7, 11, 12, 13, 14, 16, 17, 18, 32, 37, 39, 40, 43, 45, 46, 49, 52, 53, 57, 59, 60, 61, 62, 63, 64, 65, 67, 69, 70, 73; Elizabeth Whiting & Associates 54.

Illustrations: Graham Bingham 8, 9, 21, 23, 24, 25, 26, 28, 29, 30, 31, 35, 38, 41, 42, 44, 51, 52, 58, 59, 67, 69, 71.

We are grateful to Mrs Anne Ormerod and Mrs Helen Pearson for letting us photograph their homes (pp.32 and 73) and to Mrs Pauline Hunt.

Tools and materials supplied by J T Keep & Sons Limited.